WELCOME TO OUR COLOUR WORLD.

Greetings Future Artists! Are you ready to explore the Colour World with amazing experiments? And become masters of colour? Your Art will be energised with colour!

LET'S CREATE SOME COLOUR ENERGY!

COLOURS COME FROM LIGHT.

YOUR FIRST EXPERIMENT IS TO MAKE A SUN CATCHER TO LOOK **SAFELY** AT LIGHT ENERGY FROM THE SUN.

You will need:
- Cardboard box
- Sheet of white paper
- Tin foil
- Sticky tape
- Scissors
- Pin

WHAT'S INSIDE?

OOH! IT'S EVERYTHING WE NEED TO CATCH THE SUN IN A BOX!

FIRST YOU TAPE THE WHITE PAPER INSIDE THE BOX.

IS THIS THE SCREEN?

YES

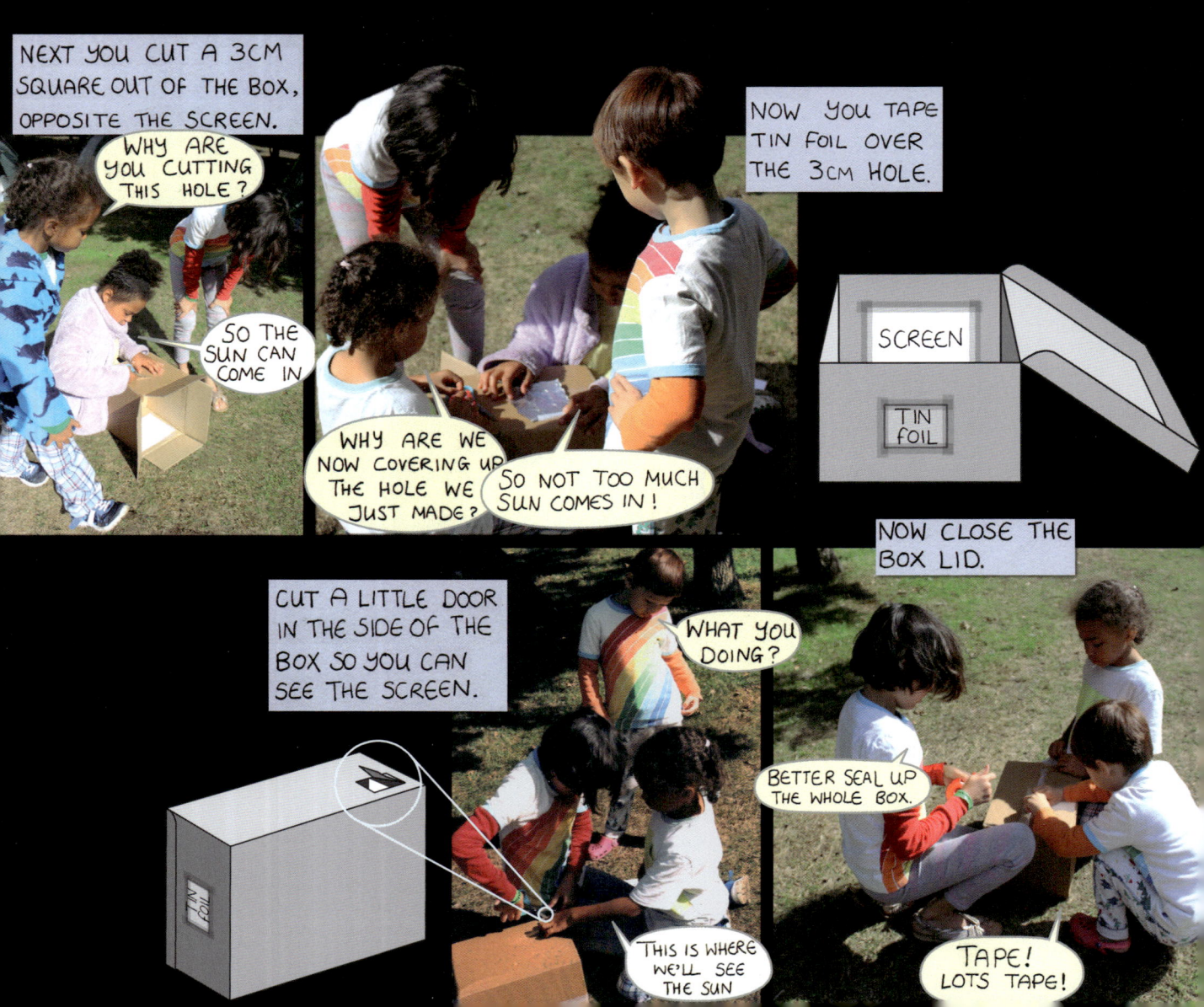

COLOUR IS LIGHT.

The Sun lights up our world with bright white light.
But the world looks colourful.

How can we see the colours in light?

"I KNOW, LET'S GO ON A RAINBOW HUNT!"

"THERE'S A RAINBOW AROUND YOU WHEN I LOOK THROUGH THE PRISM, BUT IT'S TRAPPED INSIDE"

YOU CAN MAKE YOUR OWN RAINBOWS USING A PRISM.

"WATER IN A TRAY, THAT WILL DO"

RAINBOWS COME OUT WHEN YOU HAVE LIGHT AND WATER.

WE PUT A MIRROR INSIDE TO CATCH THE SUNLIGHT...

.. NO RAINBOWS YET.

All the colours live in light. We can see all the colours if we bend sunlight in water. Light makes things colourful.

Try it yourself. Which colours can you see?

If you shake the water, what happens when the colours mix up again?

You will need:
- Plastic tub
- Water
- Mirror
- Plasticine

Hey, Colour Bestie,

Been fiddlin' with some scraps from Eddie's studio yesterday...

Check out my new favourite emoji!

10:10

Aaargh! Am I supposed to do Eddie's stare test on it? I can't stare at that for 30 seconds, it's a bit scary...

10:12

But it's lovely! Gah!

Alright, nuvver one then. Your favourite! Stare at the white spot in the middle of THIS.

Don't blame me if you get hungry!

What do you see when you stare at these pictures and then look at a white background?

10:14

> Got it. But I had to stare at the white page a bit longer. The picture appeared slowly. And I needed LOTS more light. NOW I'M HUNGRY. Can I make you one after my snack? What do you like?
> 10:21

> RAINBOWS! CATS!
> 10:22

> TA DA! I had to make this one up. They don't have rainbow cats.
> 11:34

> Can you make your own emoji pictures with colours torn out of magazines?
>
> You can use Eddie's stare test to find the different colours you want.

> LOVE IT!
> 11:36

> I'm a bit confused by some of the colours. Sometimes blue looks a bit violet. What about reddy-orange?
> 12.06

> Well, colours are like families. There's lots of them and they look a bit different and a bit the same. Like how you look a bit like your brother.
> 12:07

> BUT WE'RE NOT THE SAME.
> 12:07

COLOURS HAVE A FAMILY.

Get some old magazines and pick a colour.
Find pages with your colour on and cut them out.

We will use these scraps to make a colour family of little paper people!

COLOURS LIVE TOGETHER.

You know how some families are noisier than others? And some are so quiet. Maybe they're always at work? Well some colour families are louder than other colour families.

Make a colour family. They should all be one colour.

See how many you can fit in each room before they get too noisy.

Try and make the room and the family feel equally loud.

Compare yours with what your friends and family do.

There's no right answer, so you might get a bit noisy too!

Deciding how much of one colour to put on top of another colour is called **colour harmony**.

COLOURS ARE NEIGHBOURS.

Colours live on a Colour Street.
What is a Colour Street?
Let's make one!

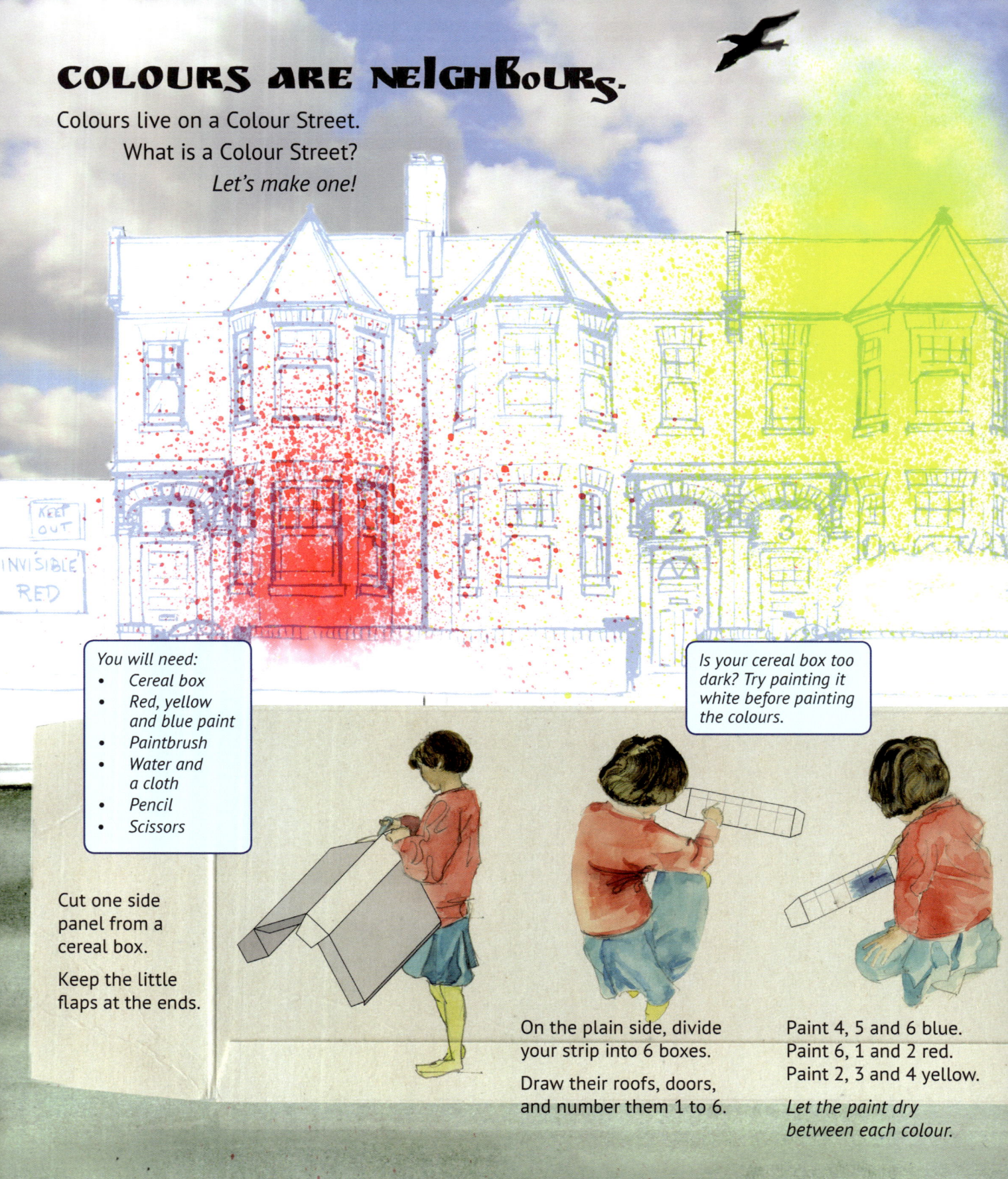

You will need:
- *Cereal box*
- *Red, yellow and blue paint*
- *Paintbrush*
- *Water and a cloth*
- *Pencil*
- *Scissors*

Is your cereal box too dark? Try painting it white before painting the colours.

Cut one side panel from a cereal box.

Keep the little flaps at the ends.

On the plain side, divide your strip into 6 boxes.

Draw their roofs, doors, and number them 1 to 6.

Paint 4, 5 and 6 blue.
Paint 6, 1 and 2 red.
Paint 2, 3 and 4 yellow.

Let the paint dry between each colour.

Ooooh. When the colours overlap it becomes a rainbow!

When we hunted rainbows, we found each colour always has the same neighbours. That's why your Colour Street looks like a rainbow!

Cut a slit halfway across your strip at both ends.

Cut one slit from the top and the other slit from the bottom.

Curl your strip around and slide the two slits together.

Hooray! Your Colour Street is now a Colour Circle!

Turn to the next page to see how your Colour Circle works.

COLOURS CAN MOVE.

Your Colour Circle can tell us about colour friendships.

Which colours are joined by this line?

These are Colour Friends. They are opposites.

Just like real life, friends are often very different to each other.

Opposites attract!

Put your Colour Circle on top of this circle.

Which colours are joined by this triangle?

These three colours go well together.

They are not best friends like the colour opposites, but they get on really well.

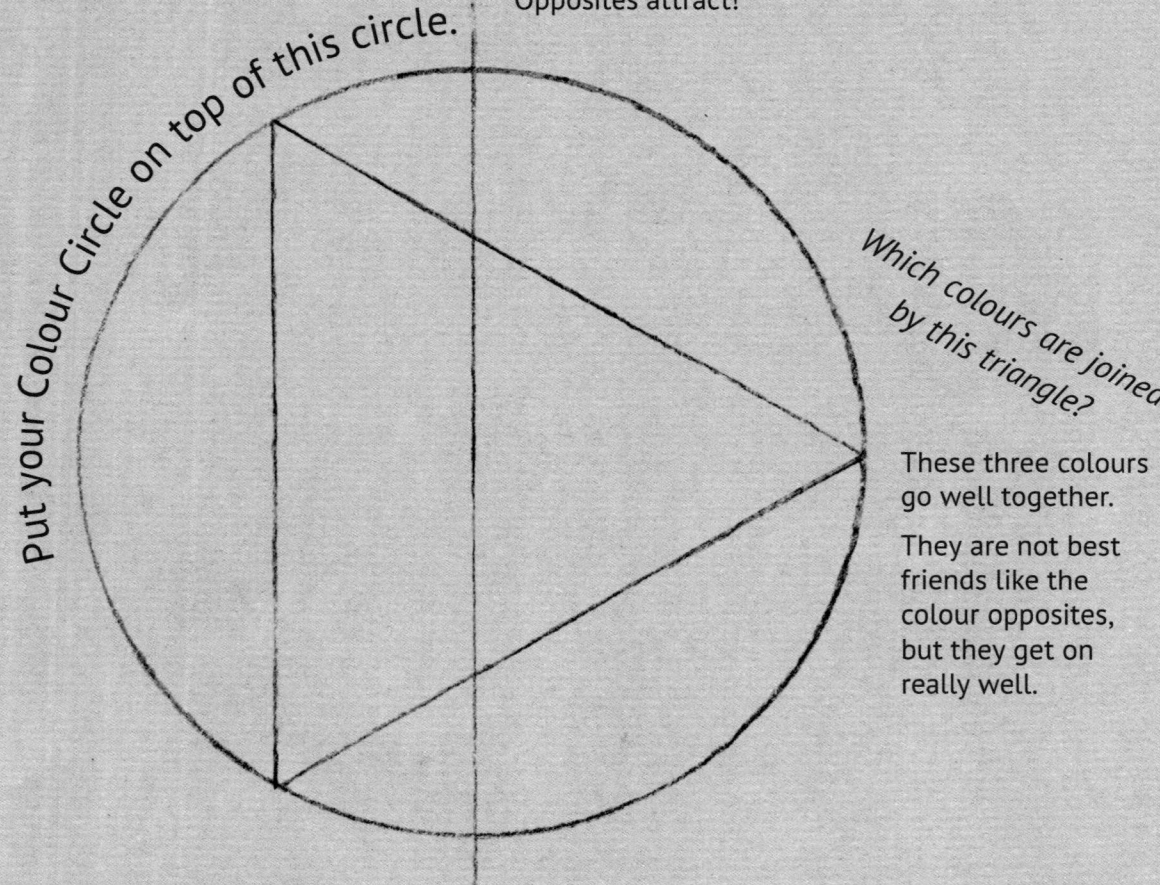

Your Colour Circle is another way of finding Colour Friends. The triangle and line tell us which colours will effect each other the most.

Your Colour Circle is also useful when you are *mixing* colours!

Mixing paint is really important. It is so important, we are going to mix our paints and not even paint anything with them!

You will need:
- Red, yellow and blue paint
- Paintbrush
- Water and a cloth
- Palette

Don't have a palette? Anything flat will do. Like the lid from a plastic takeaway box.

Every time you mix a colour, clean your brush in some water and dry it with a cloth.

This stops your colours getting muddy.

Add a little yellow paint to some red paint on your pallette.

Now look at your Colour Circle. See how red moved along the street towards yellow's house and made another colour?

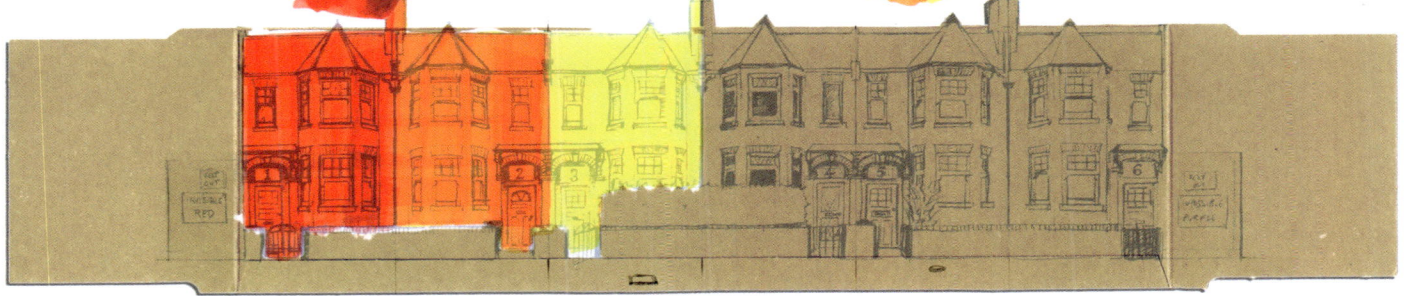

Ah! That's why orange lives between red and yellow.

Now try the same again but with blue and red.

Look at your Colour Circle. See how blue moves along the street towards red's house and makes another colour?

Oh! No wonder violet lives between blue and red.

You can move colours along their street by mixing them!

Experiment with different amounts of different colours.

See how far you can move a colour along the Colour Street. Who likes moving house and who just doesn't?

COLOURS CAN BE LIGHT OR DARK.

Colours can do more than move along their street.

Just like there is a whole world beyond the street where we live, Colours have a whole Colour Planet where all the different colours can be found!

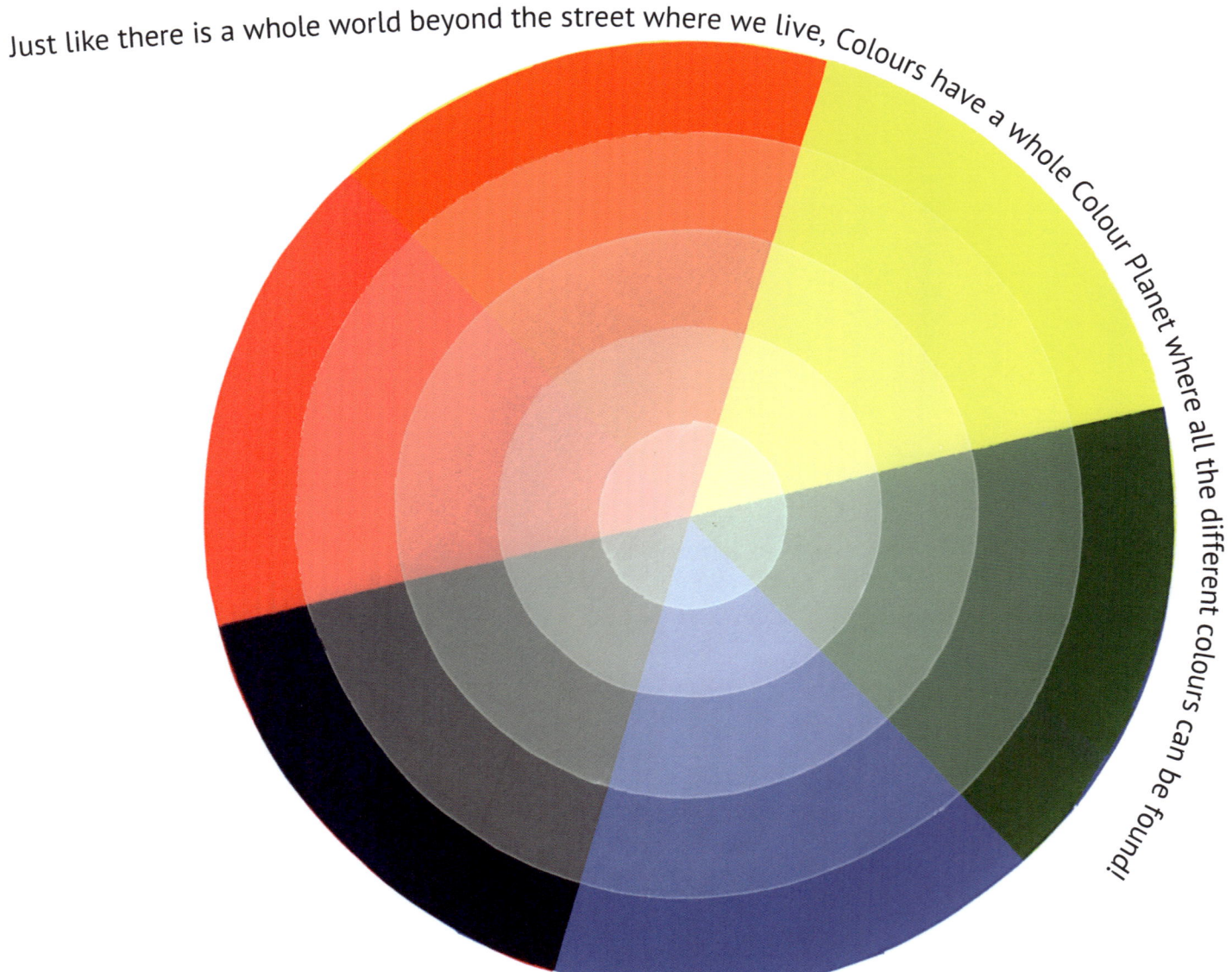

Add **white** to a colour and it gets lighter.
Artists call these light colours **Tints**.

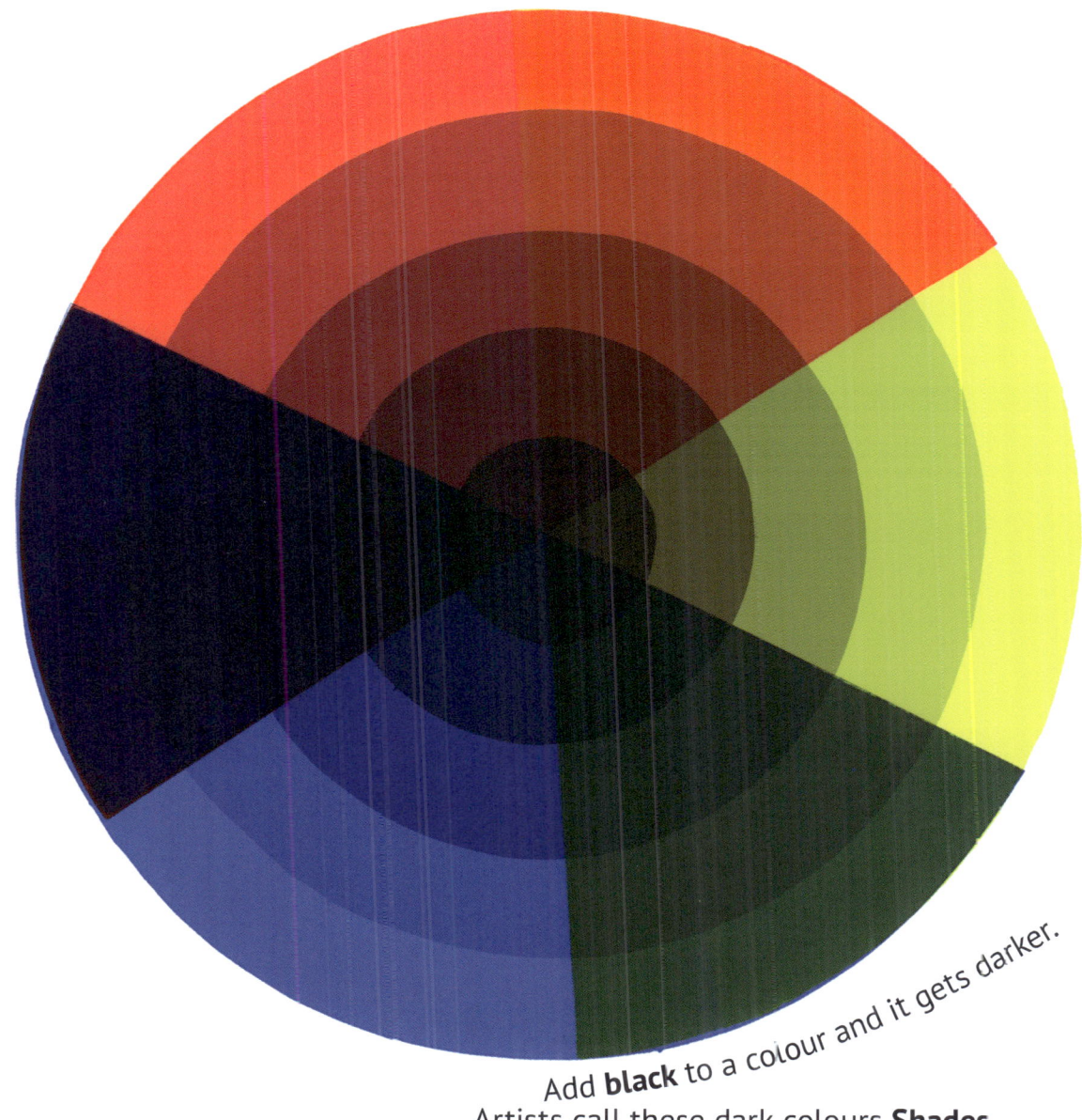

Add **black** to a colour and it gets darker.
Artists call these dark colours **Shades**.

MAKING A COLOUR PLANET.

Now we can use your new colour moving skills to make a colour planet!

You will need:
- Paint in all the colours of your Colour Street
- Paintbrush
- Palette
- Water and a Cloth
- 2 Split Pins
- Scissors
- String
- Paper

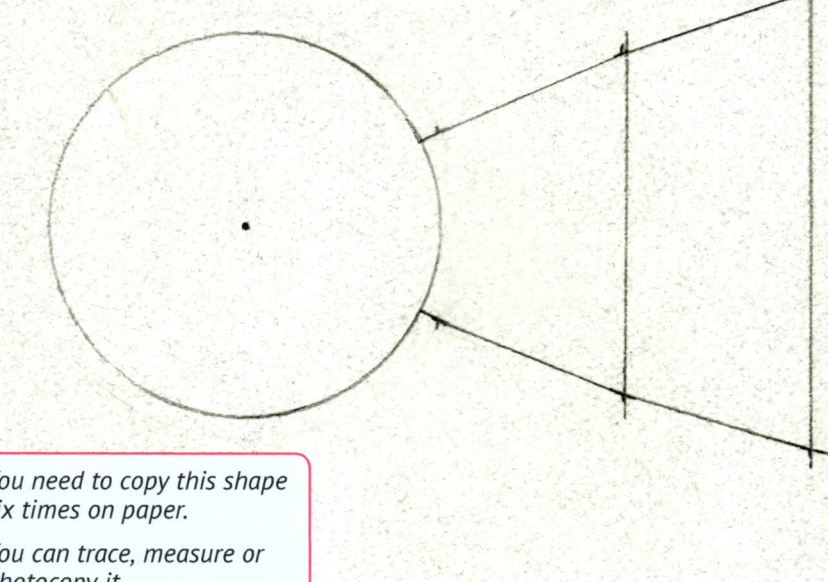

You need to copy this shape six times on paper.

You can trace, measure or photocopy it.

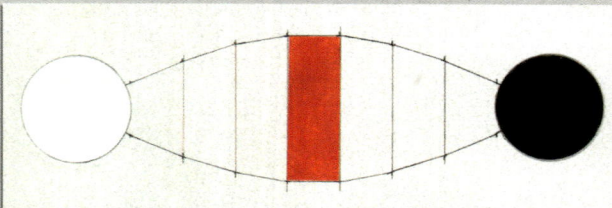

Paint **black** at one end, **white** at the other end and **red** in the middle.

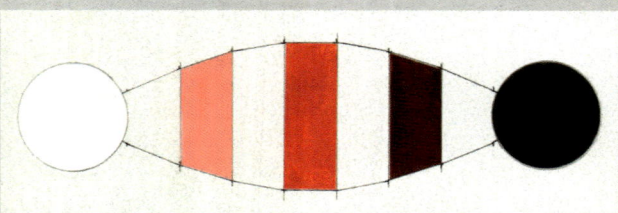

Next mix equal amounts of **white** and **red** and paint this new pink **tint** in the box halfway between them.

Mix **black** and **red** and paint the **shade** you get between them.

Your palette is where you think.

Filling the boxes with colours is like saving work on a computer.

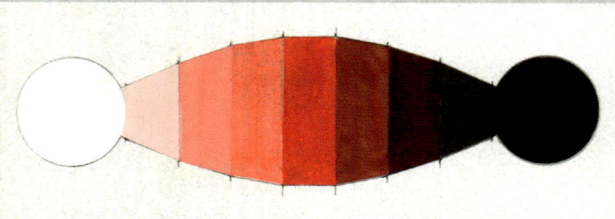

You have four empty boxes. To fill them, find the colours from either side on your palette and mix equal amounts.

Repeat the process six times.

One strip for every colour found on your colour street.

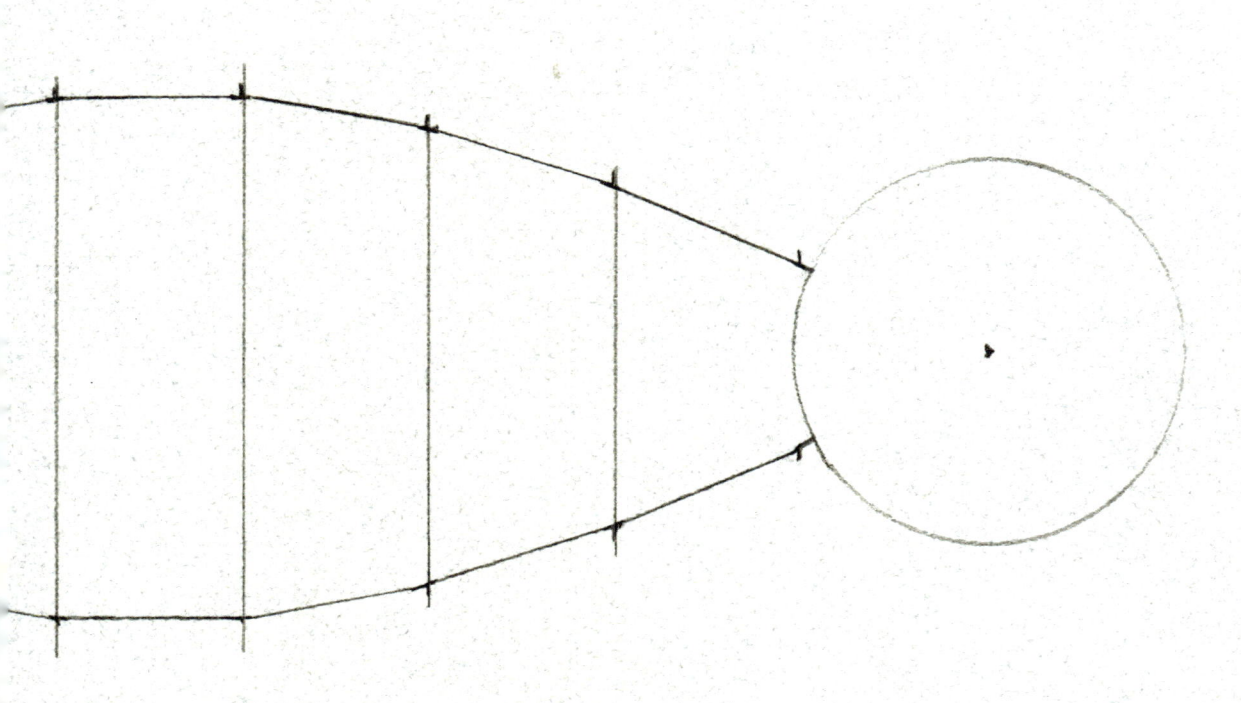

1. Cut out all the strips.
2. Poke a hole through the middle of the black and white circles. To do this safely, push your point through the paper into something squidgy.

   Not sure what to use? How about a sharpened pencil on some playdough?

3. Push a split pin through three of the black circles. Make sure the head of your pin is on the blank side. Do the same with the white circles.

   Make sure the strips are in the same order as your Colour Street.

4. Tie the pin heads together with string so the paper curves up like a bowl.
5. Put the rest of the strips on. Check again they are in the same order as your Colour Street.
6. Flatten the split pins. Done!

USING YOUR COLOUR PLANET.

How do Colour Families keep in touch with their globetrotting friends?

They talk to each other using shapes!

Imagine a line, triangle or pyramid inside your Colour Planet.

The line connects two Colour Friends living on opposite sides of the Colour Planet.

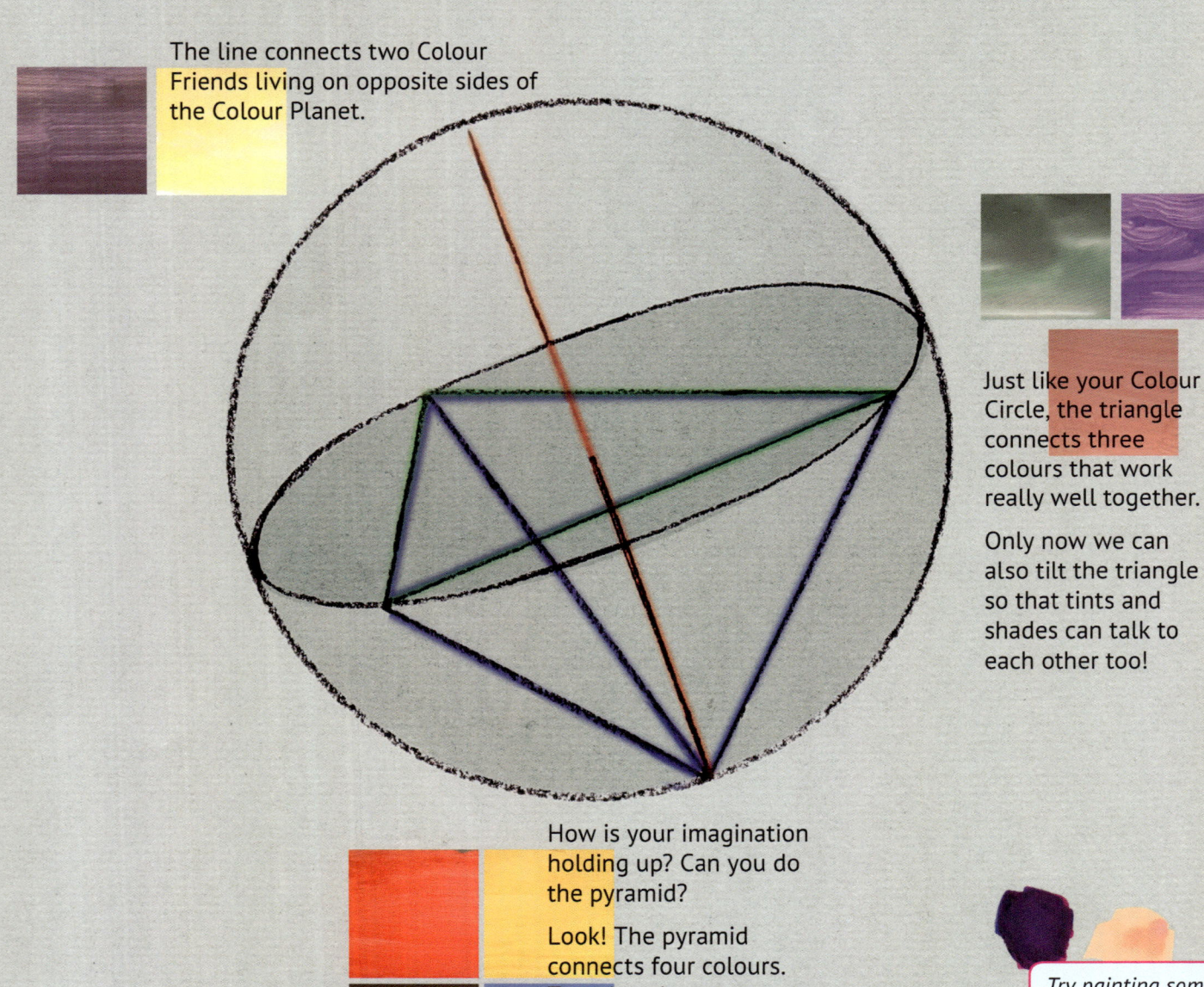

Just like your Colour Circle, the triangle connects three colours that work really well together.

Only now we can also tilt the triangle so that tints and shades can talk to each other too!

How is your imagination holding up? Can you do the pyramid?

Look! The pyramid connects four colours. Together they create a colour scheme that is out of this world!

Try painting some swatches that record your colour conversations.

COLOURS CAN BE HOT AND COLD.

Just like planet Earth, some parts of the Colour Planet feel hotter or colder than others.

We can feel a colour's temperature with our eyes!

Artists use this to mix colours that jump out or sit back on a page.

THIS GREY IS HALF BLACK AND HALF WHITE. IT'S KIND OF STUCK.

ADDING RED WARMS IT UP AND BRINGS IT FORWARD.

ADDING BLUE COOLS IT DOWN AND PUSHES IT BACK.

Colour temperature is especially useful when painting 3D shapes.

We know we can make shades by adding black. Shades sit back. They look further away because they are **dark**.

But what if you add a Colour Friend instead of black?

The colour you get looks further away because it is **cool**.

Notice how much brighter shades look when you use a Colour Friend.

AFTER OUR RAINBOW HUNT, WE MEASURED THE TEMPERATURE OF THE DIFFERENT COLOURS.

HEY! THE RED IS ACTUALLY A TINY BIT HOTTER THAN THE BLUE!

WE EVEN FOUND AN INVISIBLE COLOUR NEXT TO RED, CALLED INFRA-RED.

YOU KNOW IT IS THERE BECAUSE IT IS HOTTER THAN RED.

THERMOMETER GUN
PRISM
RAINBOW
INVISIBLE INFRA-RED

Try it yourself!

If you don't have a fancy thermometer gun, you can put two normal thermometers in your rainbow. But you need to paint their bulbs black.

COLOURS MIX MIX MIX IN YOUR IMAGINATION.

Tear open most food packets and you'll find these four colour dots.

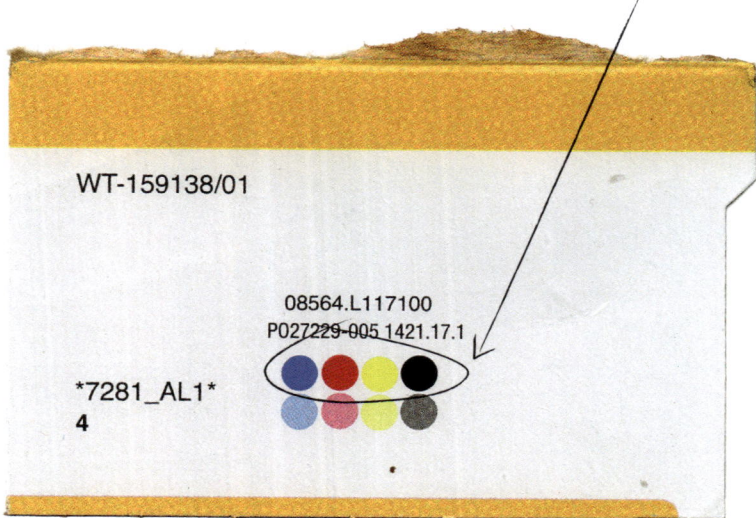

Every colour you see on the packet is printed using just these four colours. *Amazing!*

Instead of mixing colours on a palette, your eyes mix the dots in your brain!

Printers call these colours CMYK, which stands for **Cyan**, **Magenta**, **Yellow** and **Keyline**.

Black is the 'Key' used to lock all the colours together.

To make colours look darker or lighter the printer uses bigger or smaller dots.

To mix colours, the printer puts the four colours near each other in patterns called **Rosettes**, like this.

The dots go in straight lines, but together they make circles.

Can you spot small circles of dots?

Can you spot bigger circles of dots?

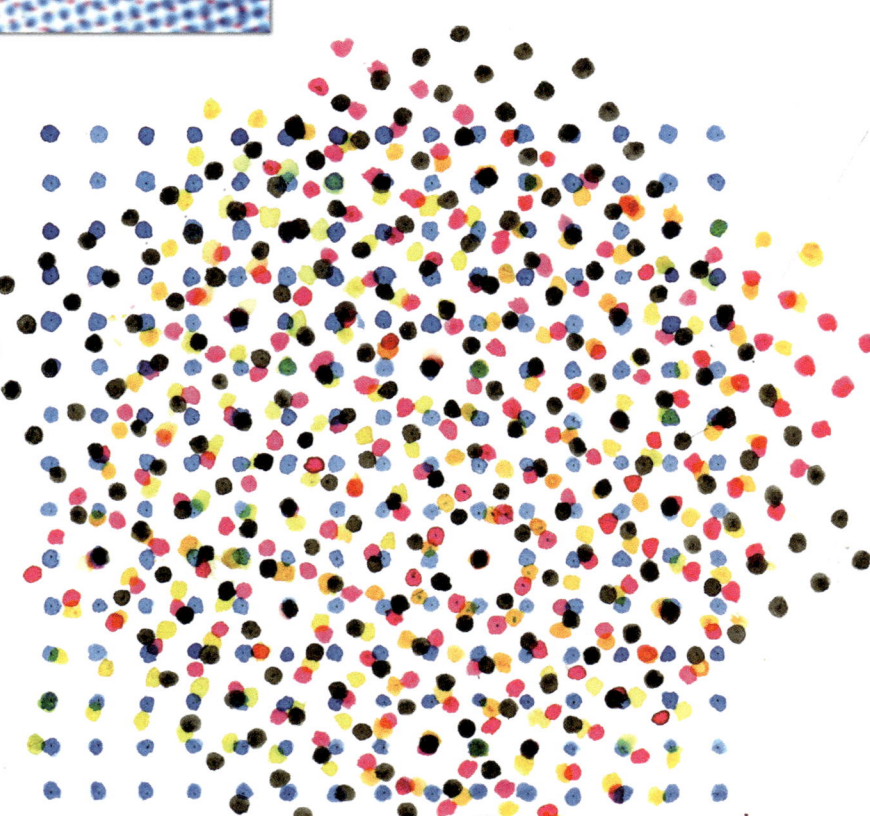

Dots can make colours. This yellow is really made of a bright yellow background with tiny magenta dots on top.

This moves the bright yellow a little bit down the colour street towards red. This makes the packet a tiny bit more orangey.

Dots can make pictures. Use a magnifying glass or camera to zoom in on the dots on your packet.

To take a sample, use a hole-punch to make a hole in a piece of paper. Put this over your packet. This helps you concentrate on just the dots.

Try enlarging the dots from your sample by drawing a big circle on paper and copying the dots into it.

What happens when you look at your big circle from far away?

All colour is an illusion. Colour begins in our eyes and ends in our imagination. There is no colour in the outside world. But colour is part of how we see the world.

When something looks blue, that means it eats the other colours and blue light bounces off.

Red things eat all the other colours. We see red light bouncing off.

Broccoli looks that colour because it won't eat its greens!

Things look black when they eat ALL the colours. White things don't eat ANY colours.

But what are they eating?

What are colours actually made of?

COLOURS ARE WAVES

Colours are just a tiny part of a family called **Electromagnetic Waves**. Every wave in this family carries energy through space.

COLOUR IS ENERGY!

No wonder colours bring so much energy to our Art. You control the energy in your artworks by using your colours!

Come meet colour's cousins. To play this game you will need one 6-sided die and a counter each.

④ **Microwaves** make the water in our food jiggle-jiggle hot. *DING! Roll again.*

① **Radio Waves** carry music and messages to our ears. *Go ahead 2 spaces.*

start

finish

WELL DONE! You're the winner. Give us a wave!

Time to zap some cells!
First player to roll 1 or 2 five times goes to the finish!

(One roll per turn)

(20) Doctors use **Gamma Rays** to BLAST cancer cells inside the human body.

9

(10) **Infra Red** waves are heat.

Bask in the toasty waves from your radiator and miss a turn.

11 12 (13) 14 15 16 17

Colour Waves are the only energy waves we can see with our eyes!

Red waves are stretched.
Blue waves are squashed.

Yellow waves... slide you back down the rainbow to 11! Ha.

(19) **X - Rays** pass through our skin to make photos of our bones.

1 or 2? Broken leg! Miss a turn.
3, 4, 5, 6? Hop on to 20.

(18) **Ultraviolet Rays** burn our skin.

Take a minute to put your sunblock on.

Roll 1 or 2 to go on to 19.